THE
HANDS
OF A
WARRIOR

Preparing Your Family for Spiritual War

A Men's 30-Day Devotional

M. A. DOZIER

Dedicated to the men who came before me
and waged war on my behalf:

For Pa,
who spiritually poured into his children
so that generations of spiritual warriors
would continue to be trained up and fight the fight.
Thank you for your eternal legacy.
I cannot wait for you to one day meet your greatgrandchildren
in the streets of heaven.

For my dad,
who took seriously his role as a spiritual leader
and who daily encouraged and strengthened me
into the man I have become. You took the time
to invest in my hobbies and interests—
and more importantly, in my soul.
Through your actions and words,
I have witnessed how to spiritually lead my own family.
Thank you for continuing the legacy.

CONTENTS

INTRODUCTION

The western church has become complacent. As men in the body of Christ, we're spiritually sleeping and have completely dismissed our duties as spiritual leaders in our home. We've claimed work and finances as our primary role there while failing to lead our children spiritually.

There's a war being waged—and the enemy is determined to steal, kill, and destroy the souls of our kids, our marriages, and our families. If we remain apathetic to our responsibilities as spiritual leaders, we'll usher our children and future generations into the abyss of eternal separation from Christ.

In this thirty-day devotional book, you'll discover what it means to be the spiritual leader you're called to be. You'll learn what armor to put on, and what weapons to fashion so you can prepare yourself, your wife, your children, and future generations for battle. This is the most important battle of your life. It will test you, exhaust you, and beat you down. But at the end of the fight, my prayer is that you'll hear these words: "Well done, my good and faithful servant."

At the end of each day's devotion, you'll be sent away with an armory of scriptures—to spur you toward dusting off your Bible and diving in. This is your training ground for the spiritual war you're surrounded by, and which is engulfing your family. But don't rely on this book. This is merely a training pamphlet for the true manual, God's Word. To be victorious in this war, you must constantly open that manual and seek wisdom from it.

I pray for conviction as you turn each page. I pray God opens your eyes to the war raging around you, and that you find urgency in the need to either begin or further sharpen the spiritual training of your family.

Are you ready?

BEFORE YOU BEGIN

We all have our own unique story. Our stories are built upon the foundations of our culture, family life, trauma, genetic makeup, religion, and more—all molding and shaping each of us into the distinctive man we are today.

At Fatherhood.org, I saw an overwhelming statistic: one in four children in America live without a father in the home. Maybe you grew up without a dad. Maybe you were tossed back and forth between homes in a split marriage. Maybe you grew up with an abusive man in the home. Maybe your father was physically present but was more involved in his own work and hobbies than in your life. Or maybe you're one of the few who was raised by a very intentional and loving father. The truth is that most of you reading this book have been hurt by your earthly dad. Your story may be written by these hurts, and some of you may be holding onto pain beyond any that I could wrap my head around. But these experiences do not define who you are.

In *The Knowledge of the Holy* A. W. Tozer writes, "What comes into our minds when we think about God is the most important thing about us."

Is your view of your heavenly Father shaped by the experiences you had with your earthly father, or is it shaped by the truth found in Scripture? My objective in asking this is not to tear you down, but to urge you toward shining the light of Jesus in your soul, to expose dark corners where the devil has built strongholds. No man is perfect. We all have blind spots, and without the supernatural intervention of Jesus in our lives, we are utter failures.

God has uniquely crafted you to be the greatest influence in your family's life, and he has equipped you to lead them spiritually. The devil wants to convince you that you're unqualified to lead your family. The devil wants to tell you that you're handicapped because of the lack of spiritual upbringing in your own life. The devil wants you to believe that someone else is better suited to spiritually pour into the lives of your children. Don't let these lies infiltrate your mind. God has ordained you and prepared you as a warrior to stand in your family's defense, and to train your children in the spiritual realms. It doesn't matter how bad you think you've messed up. It doesn't matter if you think it's too late, because your children are grown (or almost). In Christ we are new creations. He has chosen *you* to lead your family. Stand on that, immerse your soul in that, and move forward in the truth that you are the man for the job.

One of my favorite interactions in Scripture is between Job and God himself, including these words that God spoke to him: "Brace yourself like a man, because I have some questions for you, and you must answer them" (Job 38:3 NIV). One day we'll stand before the throne of the Almighty, and he will question us—and we'll have to answer like a man, and give an account for our actions.

During the next thirty days, we're going to face hard questions. We're going to wrestle with truth, and it will be abrasive. It may be offensive, and hurt our feelings. But let me share an absolute truth with you: Hell doesn't care about our feelings. Hell doesn't care about our excuses. Hell doesn't care about our opinions. Hell is concerned only with devouring our souls and everything we hold precious in our lives. If we buy the lie that our feelings and pride and ego outweigh the truth of the gospel, then we're directing our lives and our offspring toward eternal suffering.

Men in our culture have lost the ability to speak to other men with candor, forwardness, and soul-searching abrasiveness that grinds away the rust and decomposition of the world and restores life back into the heart of another man. We all need other men who are willing to do the hard work of sharpening us through tough love, so we can be effective in leading our families. We need men who will hold our hearts to the grinding wheel of the gospel, to strip us of passivity and polish us into the God-fearing leaders we were ordained to be.

I once heard my dad tell a man, "Each of us holds the power to make a decision that will forever branch our family tree in the direction of Jesus." The poor decisions of our earthly fathers do not define our legacies, so let's choose to walk in the truth of the gospel, and allow our heavenly Father to define our legacy. Let's lead with conviction and integrity. Let's go to war for the souls of our families.

1

WELCOME TO WAR

*You will receive power when the Holy Spirit has come upon you,
and you will be my witnesses in Jerusalem and in all
Judea and Samaria, and to the end of the earth.*

ACTS 1:8

The evangelical church in the western world is seeing the largest exodus of people it has ever seen. I've seen statistics in church analytics indicating that only thirteen percent of the millennial generation are actively involved in a local church, and an even smaller percentage of the Gen Z population will darken the door of a church after they turn eighteen.

What we're seeing is the product of the body of Christ becoming complacent. They're slowly fading away from biblically founded truth, drifting into the deadly lie of cultural Christianity. We see this overwhelmingly present in the United States, where for decades the majority of the population put on the badge of Christianity but never surrendered their life to the lordship of Jesus Christ. Because of this, succeeding generations have seen no practical and life-changing reason to follow Jesus. Unfortunately, the ones who raised them represented their faith as "This is something we do" rather than "This is who we are to the very fiber of our being."

Our job as men is to be our family's spiritual leaders—and we're failing in grand fashion. Our failure will reach into eternity and have consequences for generations to come unless we stand up and fight for the souls of our children.

I was having lunch with a friend who pastors a church in North Carolina, and he told me he was asked to do a funeral at a neighboring church. When he got there, he was having small talk with the pastor of the church and asked him, "So, how are things?" The pastor of the church responded, "Things are great. All my people are saved."

Here's a prime example of spiritual passivity that ultimately condemns generation after generation to the pits of hell.

Salvation is not the end goal; it is merely the beginning. But unfortunately, we as the body of Christ have bought the lie that as long as they "pray the prayer," we're all good.

Parents, I urge you: Reject this way of thought with passion and intensity!

In some of Jesus's last words before ascending into heaven, he said to his disciples (and to us), "Go and make disciples of all nations" (Matthew 28:19). We're to make disciples, but the problem is that we've assumed that a salvation prayer equals discipleship. This is simply not true.

Why is it that the majority of baptisms in our churches today are for people in middle age (or approaching it), and their typical story is, "I walked the aisle and prayed the prayer as a kid, but I had no life change"?

As a father, my job as spiritual leader doesn't end when my children become "saved." My job is to continually build them and mold them into the image of Christ. Salvation is just one step in this process. A step worth celebrating, absolutely—but it's not the end goal.

The body of Christ is suffering today because men, husbands, and fathers have vacated their role as spiritual leaders and have handed over this responsibility to others who are less qualified for the job—because God has ordained fathers to lead their families spiritually. We must examine the hearts of our children and test them against the truths of the gospel. There's nothing more frightening to me than my child standing before God's throne and hearing the Lord say, "I never knew you, depart from me" (Matthew 7:23). Let us be vigilant in the pursuit of our children, to ensure that where they rest eternally will be with the Lord. May we take nothing for granted.

I will never forget hearing about a testimony where another missionary I was working with had served as an elder of his church for over a decade, yet he had only been a Christian for 2 years. Think about that for a minute. He explained that he grew up in the church and had lived a good moral life. He was active in the church, even to the point of being selected as an elder. But one day, the realization came that he'd fooled everyone, including himself. He said his life up until that point was just about the outward appearance of living the Christian life, but he'd never fully surrendered to the power and authority of Jesus Christ.

Fathers, I don't care how well behaved your child is, or how "good" they are. I don't care that by all outward appearances your child loves the Lord, can quote Scripture, or enjoys going to church. We must test their hearts and build them up daily in the truth of God's Word. We must not take anything for granted, and assume nothing. We must reject spiritual passivity at every front. We're called to be warriors in the spiritual realm, and we've been tasked with the spiritual upbringing of our children, whose eternal lives are in our hands.

Over the next twenty-nine days, I want to walk you through what it looks like to spiritually lead your family, how to build up your children to become warriors in the kingdom of Christ, and what it looks like to leave a biblical legacy that reaches coming generations. My goal is to challenge, encourage, and inspire you to be the man God has ordained you to be—a warrior in the army of the Almighty.

Now—are you ready for war?

THE ARMORY

Hebrews 3:6

2 Timothy 2:15

1 Corinthians 11:3

THE CALLING
OF A WARRIOR

So I prophesied as I was commanded. And as I prophesied,
there was a sound, and behold, a rattling, and the bones came together,
bone to its bone. And I looked, and behold, there were sinews on them,
and flesh had come upon them, and skin had covered them.
But there was no breath in them. Then he said to me,
"Prophesy to the breath; prophesy, son of man, and say to the breath,
Thus says the Lord GOD: Come from the four winds, O breath,
and breathe on these slain, that they may live."
So I prophesied as he commanded me, and the breath came into them,
and they lived and stood on their feet, an exceedingly great army.

EZEKIEL 37:7-10

The Bible is clear. Our God does not mince words. As men, husbands, and fathers, we're called to provide, protect, and lead our families. I think we can all agree to this. So why are marriages failing? Why is society collapsing, and why are families falling apart?

The devil is crafty, and we've bought the lie that our responsibility ends where spiritual life begins. We provide our families with food, clothing, and shelter. We protect them from the harsh realities of our fallen world. We care for the future of our kids. But should we not care even more about the eternity our children will dwell in?

There's a war that rages, and the evil one looks to consume our own soul and the souls of our children. And there's no house, or amount of money, or earthly weapon, or physical comfort that can protect us. This is a spiritual war; it requires divine intervention, and we're called to be warriors in the fight.

In Ezekiel 37 we encounter a strange vision showing a valley piled with dry bones. God commanded the man Ezekiel to prophesy life and breath into these bones. "And the breath came into them, and they lived and stood on their feet, an exceedingly great army." If you've received the breath of life, then you're part of a great army much like that. It's impossible to lead in a spiritual war if you've never entered the battlefield yourself. War is ruthless, and whether or not you think so, you and your family will perish in this war unless you decide today to stand up and join the army of the Almighty.

In yesterday's devotion, we heard a pastor boast about his entire congregation being "saved." We also heard the testimony of a man who'd been a church elder for years without having truly surrendered his life to Christ. The truth is, you may be sitting there today with the same kind of bold confidence in your salvation. Or maybe you're questioning it.

I've seen a heart-wrenching statistic indicating that roughly ninety percent of those sitting in the church today are not truly saved. They've fallen into the trap that Satan has laid across most of the western world—the deception of passivity and comfortability.

We're talking about the biggest decision of your life. You must surrender all that you are and have to the authority and leadership of our king, Jesus Christ. Open your hands and surrender all your possessions—home, vehicle, finances, career, and especially your marriage and your children. Lay them all at His feet. Open your heart and surrender your plans, your thoughts, your will, your soul. Give them over to him. This is an all or nothing proposition.

Jesus said, "No one can serve two masters" (Matthew 6:24). Just to be clear, surrendering to the Lord doesn't necessarily mean you'll lose your house, your job, or your family. It just means you're relinquishing control to God, for him to use these things as he sees fit. The reality is that he may tell you to stay where you are and keep what you have. But a day may come when he may redirect your path, in order to attain his ultimate plan, and on that day you must obey and take up the call.

Without the breath of life, you are lost, depraved, and destined to eternal damnation. Let me emphasize: There are two deaths, physical and spiritual. The first is a death that no one can avoid, while the second determines where you'll spend eternity. God gives us an opportunity to join him in the fight. He made our way for this by sending Jesus to die on the cross in our place, to pay for our sins. In order to properly lead your family, you must accept that you cannot do it without Jesus. You must surrender your life to him, and he will breathe life into your bones.

If you would like to join the fight, read the prayer below. But let me be clear, this is not a prayer of just salvation, it is a prayer of full surrendering; taking all we have and laying it at the feet of Jesus.

> *"Lord, I know I'm in need of you. My family needs me to provide, protect, and lead them spiritually. To do that, I need your help. So today I'm surrendering all that I am and all that I have to your leadership. I know that I'm a sinner, and that by your death on the cross I'm being given the opportunity to join the fight against the evil that seeks to devour my very soul. Today I surrender my life to you. I'm ready to become a warrior."*

If you prayed this prayer and truly meant it, I welcome you to the army of the Almighty.

Now—it's time to get to work.

Romans 3:23

Romans 10:9-10

John 5:24

Romans 6:23

Proverbs 23:26

3

THE WAR THAT SURROUNDS US

For we do not wrestle against flesh and blood, but against the rulers, against the authorities, against the cosmic powers over this present darkness, against the spiritual forces of evil in the heavenly places. Therefore take up the whole armor of God, that you may be able to withstand in the evil day, and having done all, to stand firm.

EPHESIANS 6:12-13

I f you're going to battle, it's vital to know who and where your enemy is, and why you're fighting. Our enemy, the devil, is smart. He makes his moves and fights his war through deception in half-truths. If we aren't careful, we'll find ourselves caught up in fighting a battle that's merely a distraction.

Our fight is not with people who believe differently. Our fight is not with people who live differently. Our fight is not with people of a different descent or nationality. Our fight is not in a political realm, nor in the prosperity of a nation's ideals or heritage.

Our real fight is this: to charge into the darkness and grab hold of lost souls in the world, and to bring them to Jesus so he can save and reclaim their life for the kingdom of Christ.

I was once in a conversation about homosexuality in the LGBTQ community with a group of believers. The main focus of the discussion was on their sin and how it dishonored God. At one point my wife made a profound statement: "The problem is not their lifestyle or their actions. The problem is that they simply need Jesus."

My wife was looking past the actions of others and seeing their lost and broken heart. If you merely "fix" their sin through behavioral modification, you still have a soul destined to eternal damnation. If you introduce them to Jesus, he provides the heart transplant that begins to pump new blood into their mind and soul, changing how they think and act.

Are their actions and lifestyle sinful? Absolutely, one hundred percent. But so is our gossip, as we stand in the walls of the church and talk about them.

The problem we as sinners all have is our heart. The action of sin is just a byproduct of where the heart lies. God doesn't seek behavior modification; he seeks life change. He seeks a heart transplant that literally changes the desire of your soul.

Let's make sure we're fighting for what God desires, and not the distraction that the devil lays in our path.

No amount of legislation or political and religious influence will change the heart of a man. Only the redemptive love of Christ can do that. This goes for different religions, life decisions, cultures, and religious traditions. Our fight is to love all and introduce them to Jesus.

As the spiritual leader of our home, we've been charged with the maturity and spiritual growth of our families. We lead them into battle. Our children watch and are conditioned to the battles we choose, and they eventually take up those battles as their own.

Wisdom and discernment are treasured allies in war. Allow them to speak into your decisions. They'll always point you back to the example of Christ.

Let's stand up and break the generational curses that have stained our faith through poor decisions and traditional mindsets. Actually, let's dig deeper—and look to change more than just the behavior.

We see this idea at work in Jesus's interaction with the woman at the well, as recorded in John 4. Jesus first breaks tradition, as a Jewish man, by asking a Samaritan woman for a drink. Jews and Samaritans did not interact, much less converse. Second, she was a promiscuous woman, a sinner, with multiple past husbands. She was neck deep in sin. Yet Jesus saw her as what God created her to be: a daughter of Christ. Jesus broke barriers of tradition and religious bigotry to confront a lost soul who was desperately in need of the redemptive power of Christ.

The devil wants us to believe that if we change our behavior, we've changed the soul. But Jesus shows us something different.

The church is dying in America today because we have conditioned generation after generation to fill a seat on Sunday and hear a message, and then go into the world to "live the good Christian life"—without ever actually taking time to dig beneath the surface to test our soul. The church as a whole is requiring surface level behavior modification, but God is looking much deeper. As God once told his prophet, "The LORD sees not as man sees: man looks on the outward appearance, but the LORD looks on the heart" (1 Samuel 16:7).

My fear is that on the day of judgment, there'll be entire generations who've attended church their whole life but who on that day will hear these words that Jesus long ago warned about: "I never knew you, depart from me" (Matthew 7:23).

The devil is a crafty deceiver. His half-truths are music to the flesh but cancer to the soul. Fathers, when it comes to your children, don't believe the lie that a well-behaved child is secure in the salvation of the Lord. Instead, invest in your children's lives and examine their hearts. I would much rather have a child who tests my authority every day—but who'll rest forever in the salvation of the Lord—than a child who's well behaved but destined to eternal suffering.

As we lead our families, may we firmly plant our feet upon the truth, and break barriers by showing love, mercy, grace, and hospitality to all those who cross our path. Do not allow the devil to deceive you and tempt you into a fight that is merely a distraction.

The biggest impact you can have upon the world will happen inside the walls of your home. Let us fight the good fight and make sure we're fighting the right fight. Some fights were never meant for us!

John 13:35

1 John 3:18

1 John 4:7

1 Peter 4:8

4

THE ATTRIBUTES OF A WARRIOR

Then God said, "Let us make man in our image, after our likeness.
And let them have dominion over the fish of the sea
and over the birds of the heavens and over the livestock
and over all the earth and over every creeping
thing that creeps on the earth."

GENESIS 1:26

What defines a warrior? To what standard do we hold ourselves to as men? What are the qualities and attributes we should seek to immerse our lives with?

We should all be asking these questions, because if we don't have standards, we have no purpose, and a life without purpose is dead.

The world seems to offer many explanations and answers to these questions, but the world did not create man. Everything ever created is defined by its creator. So we must remember these words from God when he created mankind: "Let us make man in our image, after our likeness" (Genesis 1:26). The standard we're to strive for is defined by our Creator, and that standard is found in the image of God.

Since our standard is found in the image of God, therefore our standard is nothing less than perfection (as Jesus sets forth in Matthew 5:48). The hard truth is, we can never reach that standard. Does that mean God should lower his standards?

Plain and simple: NO!

That's why Jesus is necessary to our victory. Without his payment of blood on the cross, we'll never reach God's expectations. Perfection can be found only through the surrender of our lives to Christ. Once we realize and accept this truth, we can start the process of forming and transforming our lives into the likeness of Christ and begin acquiring the attributes of a warrior. Jesus promised that after he ascended into heaven, he would be sending his followers a helper, an advocate—the Holy Spirit (John 14:26).

The Holy Spirit is here to guide us, teach us, and mold us. Through him we attain the attributes of a warrior. Those attributes are identified in these verses: "The Holy Spirit produces this kind of fruit in our lives: love, joy, peace, patience, kindness, goodness, faithfulness, gentleness, and self-control. There is no law against these things!" (Galatians 5:22-23 NLT).

Consider this list of attributes. Examine your soul. Where are you succeeding? Where are you lacking? Ask God to reveal these to you as you spend time here.

The apostle Paul tells us, "Examine yourselves to see whether you are in the faith; test yourselves. Do you not realize that Christ Jesus is in you—unless, of course, you fail the test!" (2 Corinthians 13:5 NIV).

Take each attribute and look at your whole life. I recommend taking a character test to truly examine your heart. (There's an excellent and short assessment you can do quickly online at www.assess-yourself.org/surveys/.) As you inspect your soul, consider attributes that society has labeled as unmanly. I've heard many men—even men in the faith—speak against men portraying gentleness, or showing love, or saying the forbidden and apparently "weak" words "I love you." I've spoken with many men who claimed they never heard their earthly father actually say to them, "I love you." In turn, they struggle to say that to their own wives and children.

The creator of the universe—the great I Am, the Alpha and Omega, the one wearing a blood-stained robe and riding a white horse, the one with a sword coming from his mouth, and with eyes like fire, the one who rules all nations with an iron rod—this one openly and daily tells each of us, "I love you"—just as he expresses to his people in this passage: "You are precious in my eyes, and honored, and I love you" (Isaiah 43:4).

So what's your excuse?

My prayer is that men can begin to become transparent and honest with themselves on who they really are and where they really stand. Each one of us has flaws; let's own up to them, expose them, and seek to overcome them. You may claim to excel in self-control, and because of this your home is good, your finances are good, your marriage, work, and attitude are good. By all outward appearances, you're solid in the virtue of self-control. But let's dig deeper. Are you self-controlled in your thoughts? Maybe you can bridle your tongue and fool your peers, but God sees past the facade you create. He sees who you truly are—your innermost thoughts and what you choose to do when nobody else can see you. A true warrior looks to change not just his flesh, but more importantly his soul—the core of who he is. He allows God to strip away the old and replace it with the new and holy and righteous attributes of God.

We're told in God's Word, "Do not lie to each other, since you have taken off your old self with its practices and have put on the new self, which is being renewed in knowledge in the image of its Creator" (Colossians 3:9-10 NIV).

The makings of a warrior begin in the crushing of a man.

Psalm 119:9-16

Psalm 139:23-24

5

A WARRIOR DOES NOT FIGHT ALONE

Be devoted to one another in love.
Honor one another above yourselves.

ROMANS 12:10 NIV

The devil is trying to dismantle the foundation of the family unit. If he can break up a family, he can drastically decrease the chance of those children being discipled for the gospel of Christ. The number one way he attacks the family is through infiltrating our marriage. If we fail to acknowledge these advances of the enemy, by the time we realize what's happening, it will be too late.

As believers, our marriage is a living example of Christ's love for the church to the world around us. Men, we are called to love our wives as Christ loves the church—and Scripture tells us that Jesus humbled himself to the point of death on the cross for the church. Husbands, are we humbling ourselves in service to our wives—even to the point of death?

One of the greatest ways—perhaps *the* greatest way—that we can spiritually lead our families is in how well we love our wives. Our children will learn how to fight for and strengthen their own marriages based on how we live in ours. Simply by seeing how we love our wives, our children will learn how to love and to know that they themselves are loved.

In Genesis, we see that the first man Adam was around only a short while before God decided it wasn't good for a man to be alone. So after he was created, God said, "I will make a helper fit for him" (Genesis 2:18).

We cannot become the men God calls us to be without the support of our wives. In God's perfect design, our wives were created to encourage, support, and push us to lead our families well. They've been uniquely designed to build us into the God-fearing men our children desperately need. But for them to do that, we must take the time and invest in them, in who God created them to be.

When we get married, Scripture tells us that we become one flesh with our wives. We're no longer two separate individuals living solo lives; we become one singular unit. This requires us to drop our pride and our desires and place them on the table. Then together husband and wife begin to formulate a plan to work in harmony for the glory of God. This is not easy. It's a major arena in which the devil takes hold of our marriages as he whispers lies into our souls, trying to get us to reclaim our individual self. He says things like "You deserve better," or "She's not being fair," or "Other men's wives let them get away with things like this." We must rebuke those lies immediately, or they'll begin to fester and grow seeds of contempt and jealousy in our hearts.

I've seen the marriages of dear friends fall apart. Each situation had a long list of issues that both individuals needed to repent of. But in looking at just the husbands in these situations, I've found a common fault that I believe is all too typical among men: We're neglecting our wives. We're doing what *we* want, when we want. We're isolating our wives and leaving them behind. We make the excuse about job stress or our consuming hobbies, and we spend time with our wives only when our schedule allows it.

One divorced buddy of mine has admitted that when he got married, he lived his life with no consideration to the wants and needs of his wife. If he wanted to go deer hunting, or hit the gym, or hang out with the guys, he did just as he pleased. The day his wife handed him the divorce papers, he was shocked. He honestly thought things were great, but he was oblivious to the needs of his wife, and he failed to humble himself and love and serve her as Christ does for the church. Their marriage lasted barely two years.

We must acknowledge that without our wives right beside us, we cannot fully lead our families spiritually. I depend and rely on my wife and her wisdom and her discernment on a daily basis. I'm called to lead, but she's my number one adviser in this war that seeks to burn my family to the ground.

Men, if you're single, find yourself a God-fearing woman to marry who will speak truth into your soul and push you to love God more and more each day. Then love her unconditionally, and prioritize her as God sees her. She is royalty. She's a queen in the courts of the Almighty.

And if you're married, but your marriage is crumbling to the ground, you must plead for God to intercede. You must pray that he will give you a heart that's willing to drop your pride, to prioritize your wife, and to begin loving her unconditionally in whatever way she receives love best. Do this even if you think she's at fault. We all sin often, and it hurts our Father, yet he still meets us face to face at the cross. He dropped everything to love us unconditionally, even in our worst moments—and we must do the same if we choose to win victory in our marriage.

Are we loving our wives as Christ loved the church?

Together, you can wage a war that will one day build a legacy that reaches into eternity, reclaiming souls out of the darkness and bringing them into the light of truth found only in the salvation given by Jesus Christ.

THE ARMORY

Ecclesiastes 4:9-12

Genesis 2:18-24

Song of Songs 8:6-7

Colossians 3:14-17

Ephesians 4:23

6

FORGING A WARRIOR

This day the LORD will deliver you into my hand,
and I will strike you down and cut off your head.

1 SAMUEL 17:46

When we talk about famous warriors of the faith, we often talk about their defining moment—Elijah calling down fire, Moses parting the Red Sea, Joshua conquering Jericho, David defeating Goliath. We use those successes to highlight these men's ability to follow God. But what we miss is how God forged them years earlier into men who could complete the task in the here and now. Their victories are awe-inspiring and legendary, but those victories did not make them warriors. God had already forged them into warriors, so that at the moment of need they were confident and prepared to complete the task at hand.

We see this at a certain critical moment in the story of David and Goliath:

> And Saul said to David, "You are not able to go against this Philistine to fight with him, for you are but a youth, and he has been a man of war from his youth." But David said to Saul, "Your servant used to keep sheep for his father. And when there came a lion, or a bear, and took a lamb from the flock, I went after him and struck him and delivered it out

of his mouth. And if he arose against me, I caught him by his beard and struck him and killed him. Your servant has struck down both lions and bears, and this uncircumcised Philistine shall be like one of them, for he has defied the armies of the living God." (1 Samuel 17:33-36)

David was willing to take on the huge task of defeating Goliath, and he stepped forward ready for battle with a preparedness that came from other life experiences God used to forge him into the man God needed in that moment. God had prepared him for his time of greatness during a time in his life when he, as a mere shepherd boy, might have felt insignificant.

Have you ever thought about the process of making a knife? A blacksmith takes a raw, unformed, useless piece of metal, throws it into a furnace, and lets it sit in 1,650-degree heat. That metal gets so hot it becomes malleable. The blacksmith then takes the metal and begins to beat it with a hammer to start the forming process. This process of heating and hammering is repeated over and over until the blacksmith has formed the metal into the desired shape. Once the metal has cooled and hardened, the blacksmith takes the metal to the grinding wheel and begins to grind away on the edges, ultimately sharpening it into a blade. It's important for the knife to be sharp; a dull blade is like lukewarm coffee—a travesty. As Jesus said, "Because you are lukewarm—neither hot nor cold—I will spit you out of my mouth" (Revelation 3:16).

We as men are like raw chunks of metal. We are hard, unformed, useless blocks, but when we surrender to Christ and allow him to work on us and form us, we see a different outcome. We become sharp, dangerous, and deadly in the war against the devil and his demons. He forms us into the men we need to be, so that we can accomplish the tasks he has ordained for us.

The midst of the battle is not the time to start training. A warrior trains and prepares, so that when the war is at his doorstep, he is confident, prepared, and ready to fight. Make no mistake: War does not discriminate. If you aren't prepared, it will devour you.

I think it's especially important to look again at how David approached his battle with Goliath. Let's focus on the confidence David had. Listen to what he goes on to say in his answer to King Saul: "The LORD who delivered me from the paw of the lion and paw of the bear will deliver me from the hand of the Philistine" (1 Samuel 17:37). Notice where David's confidence is placed. *In the Lord!*

We see this again later in David's defiant words to Goliath:

> You come to me with a sword and with a spear and with a javelin, but I come to you in the name of the LORD of hosts, the God of the armies of Israel, whom you have defied. This day the LORD will deliver you into my hand...that all the earth may know that there is a God in Israel. (17:45-46)

David gives all credit to God. He knew his only chance of victory lay in the hands of the Lord. David had it figured out: *All glory to God!* Even after he'd chased down lions and bears, he still had the humility to understand that his victories were found in the power of God, and God alone.

Pay attention here, because all men are guilty of self-glory to some level. The Lord provides victory, and we begin to claim it as our own. We begin to take credit, but we are powerless without Christ. Any shred of success you think you can claim personally is a facade and a disgrace to the name of Christ. Without Christ in our lives, we are useless lumps of metal, and our pride is the number one hindrance to us being forged into warriors. We are weak, flawed vessels that self-destruct a hundred percent of the time when left in charge of our own lives. To reach the mountaintop, we must surrender to Christ in the valley. *Own this, accept it, embrace it— never forget it!*

Paul tells us of his experience in being weak and harassed, and how the Lord at that time said to him, "My grace is sufficient for you, for my power is made perfect in weakness"; Paul then goes on to confess, "Therefore, I will boast all the more gladly of my weaknesses, so that the power of Christ may rest upon me" (2 Corinthians 12:9).

It's time we tap into the power of Christ and his redemptive blood on the cross. It's time we surrender our lives to him and allow him to forge us and sharpen us into warriors, so he can slay the enemy giants we encounter, and cut off their heads!

Matthew 16:24

Hebrews 11:6

Matthew 7:21

7

ENLISTING YOUR
DEMON-SLAYERS

Three of the thirty chief men went down and came about harvest time to David
at the cave of Adullam, when a band of Philistines
was encamped in the Valley of Rephaim.
David was then in the stronghold, and the garrison of the Philistines
was then at Bethlehem.
And David said longingly, "Oh, that someone would give me water to drink
from the well of Bethlehem that is by the gate!"
Then the three mighty men broke through the camp of the Philistines
and drew water out of the well of Bethlehem that was by the gate
and carried and brought it to David. But he would not drink of it.
He poured it out to the LORD.

2 SAMUEL 23:13-16

There's nothing like an evening out with the guys. Or a dudes' weekend to recharge the batteries. We as men crave it. When I'm stressed, exhausted, stuck in a rut, and need to clear my head, a cabin, a firepit, piles of red meat, guns, fishing poles, and the musk of testosterone filling my nose is just what the doctor ordered. Maybe your prescription looks a bit different, but we all enjoy time with the guys.

But gentlemen, let's be real. When it comes to the spiritual side of our lives, we shut down and revert to being lone wolves. We isolate and grow stagnant in our relationship with God. When we do this, we begin to lose our edge, and we become dull.

"Iron sharpens iron, and one man sharpens another" (Proverbs 27:17). As men, we're called to be warriors for the kingdom, yet I constantly see men—husbands and fathers—fading away and drowning in an ocean of passivity and apathy. We're losing the fight because men are relinquishing their God-ordained responsibility to love, lead, protect, and serve the world around them. This often seems to start with their wife and kids.

We were never meant to do life alone. The devil likes to attack our pride and tell us that if we expose our shortcomings to other men, we'll be seen as weak, and as failures. Do not buy that lie! Our strength comes in numbers, our confidence in battle comes from accountability, and with many advisers we can effectively wage our war. "So don't go to war without wise guidance; victory depends on having many advisers" (Proverbs 24:6 NLT).

The devil wants to divide and conquer. If he can break our wall of defense that protects our soul, he can also begin to infiltrate our home, our marriage, our relationships, our church, and our entire life, and burn it all down starting from the inside. Sadly, the number one way he does this is by getting us alone and isolated in our fight.

In 2 Samuel 23 we see King David in a time of war. Three of his mighty warriors come to speak with him. He tells them that he's thirsty and desires a drink from the well in Bethlehem that's behind enemy lines. Then the three mighty warriors broke through the Philistine lines and drew water from the well and brought it back to him. King David had three warriors who were willing to cross into enemy territory and bring him back this water. What's the significance of all this?

Sometimes we get so caught up in our own war, we forget to nourish our souls with the living water offered to us by Jesus Christ. We need men in our lives who'll cross into enemy lines and bring us the living water that will replenish our souls with the truth from the Word of God. David knew there was only one well with the water to truly quench his thirst. The same goes for us. The only well that our souls should drink from is the well of God's Word. The world has many wells, but they're all poisoned by the enemy, and spit in by society.

I was invited to participate in a pastors' retreat where we hog-hunted, fished, golfed, and sat around the fire. We talked often about Jesus. The retreat was hosted by Pastor Joby Martin and his church in Jacksonville, Florida. Around the third night, as we sat around the fire, one of the pastors asked Joby how he handled the stress of the job and all the distractions and jabs from the devil. He confidently responded, "I have surrounded myself with the greatest demon-slayers I could find, and they go to war for me."

Let me ask you: Do you have men like this in your life? Men who are willing to go to war for you? Men who'll cross enemy lines and deliver water from the well of truth when the war rages fiercely around you? Do you have men who'll correct you, who'll tell you when you're wrong, and who'll give you a biblical beat-down in the name of Jesus when you need it? Do you have men who'll fight for your marriage, fight for your character and integrity, and fight for your soul? Do you have men who'll fight for you in the spiritual realms even when you're knocked down and cannot fight for yourself? If not, then begin to pray that God will bring forth these men.

We were never meant to do life alone. It's time we have conversations with brothers in Christ we can trust, and ask them to wage war on our behalf. It's time we enlist our demon-slayers.

THE ARMORY

1 Thessalonians 5:11

1 Peter 3:8

Galatians 6:2

1 Corinthians 14:26

8

THE FIRST STEP IN WAR

*Hezekiah received the letter from the hand of the messengers and read it;
and Hezekiah went up to the house of the LORD and spread it before the LORD.
And Hezekiah prayed to the LORD.*

ISAIAH 37:14-15

We can train, plan, and prepare for war, but unless we step onto the battlefield, we're useless in the fight. God has called every one of us to the fight. He has ordained us as men to be the spiritual leaders to fight for the souls of our children and train them to become warriors in the kingdom of Christ. If we become apathetic in this role, we hand over our children and generations to come into a darkened world that will swallow them up and enslave them.

When running a race, the most important step is the first one. You cannot move forward until you take that first step.

So what's our first step in waging war? It's giving our fight to the Lord.

In the book of the prophet Isaiah, we read about war coming against the cities of Judah from the king of Assyria. King Hezekiah was clearly stressed about this: "As soon as King Hezekiah heard it, he tore his clothes and covered himself with sackcloth" (Isaiah 37:1).

War isn't something you look for. The reality is, war will show up at your doorstep unannounced, seeking to burn you and your family to the ground. When that day comes, how do you react? What is your natural first reaction?

As we continue reading the story, we see King Hezekiah making a move that most men would never make. The problem most men have is that we're reactionary; we don't take time to process what's happening around us before we dive full bore into the situation, consequently causing more damage than good. But King Hezekiah made one of the most profoundly wise decisions ever made in a time of war. His first action was to take the message of destruction from the king of Assyria and spread it before the Lord, and to pray (Isaiah 37:14-15). *He prayed!* King Hezekiah acknowledged that in any battle, victory is found in the Lord.

So here's the big question: When it comes to waging war on behalf of your wife, your children, and your family, have you given them to the Lord and prayed for their souls' deliverance? Have you prayed over them, allowing them to audibly hear your voice lifting them up to the creator of the universe, asking for victory in the war?

You cannot fathom the power and weight your words hold in the life of your children. Do they unequivocally know that their father on earth loves them so much that he intentionally takes time to come to the throne of the Almighty, pleading and interceding for victory on their behalf? When it comes to future generations, have they heard and experienced your prayers enough that they too can confidently pray over their own spouse and children?

This is where our fight begins. We must humble ourselves at the feet of Jesus and pray for victory, and we must prepare our children for the battles they'll one day face. As the apostle Peter instructs us, "Humble yourselves, therefore, under the mighty hand of God so that at the proper time he may exalt you" (1 Peter 5:6).

Philippians 4:6

1 Thessalonians 5:17

Jeremiah 33:3

9

A WARRIOR NEEDS A RABBI

Fear the LORD your God, you and your son and your son's son,
by keeping all his statutes and his commandments, which I command you,
all the days of your life...that your days may be long.

DEUTERONOMY 6:2

Different cultures call them by different names. But they're all the same. Karate Kid had Mr. Miyagi, Batman had Ra's al Ghul—and your children have you.

If you have children or you plan on having kids, it's imperative that you understand that God has ordained responsibilities in their life. As fathers, we've been tasked with the spiritual upbringing of our children. We're tasked with being their rabbi (which means teacher). If you feel underqualified, don't buy the lie. No one is more qualified to raise your child than you, and God has uniquely and expertly given you all the tools you need to raise your child spiritually.

In our culture today, and even in the church, we have parents subletting their responsibilities to "professionals"—a Sunday school teacher, youth pastor, small group leader, and even lead pastor. However, those people are not responsible for the spiritual health and upbringing of your child. That job was created for *you*!

One day you will stand before the Lord, and He will ask you to give an account for your wife and children. Do you think the excuse "The youth pastor didn't spend enough time with my kid" is going to satisfy the requirements God has given you?

Most men are great at being the provider and protector for their family in the physical realm. But what good is it if your kids grow up in a great home with three square meals a day and the newest kicks, but are destined to hell because we as fathers have neglected to protect their souls and provide for them spiritually? We're to train them to be warriors in the kingdom of Christ.

Spiritually leading our children is a moment-by-moment process, as we see in this passage:

> Now this is the commandment—the statutes and the rules—that the LORD your God commanded me to teach you, that you may do them in the land to which you are going over, to possess it, that you may fear the LORD your God, you and your son and your son's son, by keeping all his statutes and his commandments, which I command you, all the days of your life, and that your days may be long. Hear therefore, O Israel, and be careful to do them, that it may go well with you, and that you may multiply greatly, as the Lord, the God of your fathers, has promised you, in a land flowing with milk and honey. Hear, O Israel: The Lord our God, the Lord is one. You shall love the Lord your God with all your heart and with all your soul and with all your might. And these words that I command you today shall be on your heart. You shall teach them diligently to your children and

shall talk of them when you sit in your house, and when you walk by the way, and when you lie down, and when you rise. You shall bind them as a sign on your hand, and they shall be as frontlets between your eyes. You shall write them on the doorposts of your house and on your gates. (Deuteronomy 6:19)

When you rise, when you walk, when you sit, and *when you lie down*—at all times, we're to make the values of the Lord visible in our lives so that our children can tangibly see them and follow in our footsteps.

Fathers, the power you possess to influence your children is immeasurable. Will you use it to push them toward Christ— or away from him? Your children will never do what you tell them; they will do what you *show* them by your life. Jesus spoke about this: "Truly, truly, I say to you, the Son can do nothing of his own accord, but only what he sees the Father doing. For whatever the Father does, that the Son does likewise" (John 5:19).

Do your actions and words work in harmony to present a life that's pursuing Jesus? Is your life building a spiritual foundation that your kids can stand on? Or are you just a Sunday morning seat-filler who gives God lip service? Jesus speaks to those Sunday morning seat-fillers in these words:

Not everyone who says to me, "Lord, Lord," will enter the kingdom of heaven, but the one who does the will of my Father who is in heaven. On that day many will say to me, "Lord, Lord, did we not prophesy in your name, and cast out demons in your name, and do many mighty works in your name?" And then will I declare to them, "I never

knew you; depart from me, you workers of lawlessness."
(Matthew 7:21-23)

Let's take hold of our responsibility as fathers and pour into our kid's spiritual lives, and raise them to be warriors ready for battle. Let's be prepared to charge the gates of hell and rescue others from darkness. We're to pass the heritage of living for Christ to our children; this is the will of the Lord.

Proverbs 22:6

Exodus 18:20

2 Timothy 3:16

Romans 15:4

10

A WARRIOR NEEDS PURPOSE

*We are his workmanship, created in Christ Jesus for good works,
which God prepared beforehand, that we should walk in them.*

EPHESIANS 2:10

Have you ever been working on something and asked, "Why am I doing this? Does it even matter?" I think we've all asked that question at some point. Asking it reveals an aspect of our spiritual life that we long to fulfill. Do we have purpose in this life, or were we created just to live and then die?

I firmly believe that the reason we see so many kids in their teens and twenties walking away from the church is that God created them to fulfill a purpose in their life, and their soul longs to walk in that purpose—but we as parents have never told them that God created them for a purpose, or helped them discover that purpose. So they wander into the world in search of anything to try and fill the void.

Surveys report that two-thirds of American millennials do not regularly attend a church. Yet one of the biggest conductors driving the millennial generation is the desire to feel needed and to have a purpose. Parents, we have failed. We've raised children who deeply want to have purpose in their lives, but who have never been told that their purpose is found in Christ.

In Ephesians 2:10, Paul says that we're God's handiwork, and that we were created to do good works that God prepared for us in advance. In Isaiah 43:7 we read that God's people were created for his glory. In Jeremiah 29:11, we're told that God knows the plans for our lives.

God created us all with purpose. Yet we often go through life never pursuing that purpose, or having someone love on us enough to help us discover that purpose.

When Jesus was about to be lifted into heaven, he knew that he had to give the disciples a sense of purpose. Otherwise they would just sit around, and the world would eventually perish, not knowing about him. So Jesus gave them their purpose—and ours:

> All authority in heaven and on earth has been given to me. Go therefore and make disciples of all nations, baptizing them in the name of the Father and of the Son and of the Holy Spirit, teaching them to observe all that I have commanded you. And behold, I am with you always, to the end of the age. (Matthew 28:18-20).

The one thing we as parents should be asking is this: Are we just leading our kids to the cross and then leaving them there? Or do we lead them to the cross and then continually walk alongside them, guiding them as they search for their God-given purpose?

We've become nonchalant in our relationship with God, and our kids see the church as a country club rather than as God's army strategizing how to rescue more and more souls from the grasp of the devil. If we don't redirect our focus, we'll continue losing ground, generation after generation.

We must begin to teach our children that they're fearfully and wonderfully made, and that they serve a mighty purpose in the kingdom of Christ.

THE ARMORY

Proverbs 22:6

Exodus 18:20

2 Timothy 3:16

Romans 15:4

11

WARRIORS NEED TO KNOW THEIR LINEAGE

His offspring will be mighty in the land;
the generation of the upright will be blessed.

PSALM 112:2

It has been said before that if you don't know where you came from, how will you know where you're going?

There's a lot of truth in that statement, and as we raise our children and pour into them spiritually, it's important that we share with them their lineage.

As our kids grow and begin to experience the world around them, they'll soon discover that life is hard and not some bed of roses. By default, we're all ignorant to the reality of life when we're young. But what a blessing it is when we have someone take us under their wing and impart wisdom into our lives.

The same is true for our spiritual lives. As fathers, we're called to be the one who spiritually guides our children. One of the most influential impacts you can have on your child is sharing your testimony with them. Your story allows them to see what God has done in your life, and it gives them a glimpse of where they came from. They can trace their lineage of faith, and it becomes tangible for them—something they can begin to build on and make their own.

I can remember as a teenager trying to wade through physical and spiritual issues and situations in my own life. I remember feeling like I was on an island by myself, an outcast in a way. I think my dad could sense my struggle, and he pulled me aside one day to share something that would completely change my trajectory. "Hey, son," he said. "If you ever have questions or doubts in life or in your faith, you can always come to me, and we'll work through it together."

My dad made good on that commitment, and he often referenced his personal life and how Christ changed him. He wasn't afraid of the big questions, and if I raised a question he couldn't answer, he always took time to investigate it, and would bring forth his findings a day or two later. He always held up his end.

I think one of the biggest impacts in my life was his ability to counsel me instead of correcting me. He never once told me not to ask those questions or to change my way of thinking. He also never told me I was wrong. He would simply open his Bible and say, "Let's see what God has to say about it."

Because I knew his story and how he came to Christ, I never felt that he judged me. He never made me feel bad or talked me down. Instead, he guided me with love and wisdom from a place of knowledge and experience.

One of the most cherished items I have is a letter my grandfather wrote to my dad on the day of my birth. My grandad wrote about his faith and how children were a blessing from the Lord. He then prayed blessings over me and asked God to allow me to grow up into a God-fearing man. I cannot tell you the amount of pride and honor that overtook me as I read that letter for the first time.

If we allow our kids to see their spiritual lineage and how God has worked through the generations, it empowers them to step up with full confidence in the Lord and what He will do.

As parents, we'll get much better results if we humble ourselves and walk with our kids rather than barking orders from the sidelines. No one likes an armchair quarterback. Get involved in your child's life and allow them the privilege to get to know you and how God has worked in your life. We should allow our kids to know that God cares for them by telling them how he has cared for us.

I challenge you today to write out your testimony for your children—your personal faith story. If you struggle to identify how God has changed your heart and the moment you completely surrendered it all to him, then I urge you to pray and ask God to reveal himself to you. (Jump back to "The Calling of a Warrior" in Day 2 of this book, and pray through the prayer at the end.)

Maybe today is the day your family's lineage unfolds, and your family tree begins to branch toward Christ. If you've come to the Lord in prayer with true faith in Jesus Christ for salvation, then you've begun an eternal lineage that you now have the opportunity to spread through your family for generations to come.

"You are a chosen race, a royal priesthood, a holy nation, a people for his own possession, that you may proclaim the excellencies of him who called you out of darkness into his marvelous light" (I Peter 2:9).

Psalm 119:111

Psalm 66:16

1 John 5:11

Daniel 4:2

12

A WARRIOR'S WEAPON

For the word of God is living and active,
sharper than any two-edged sword,
piercing to the division of soul and of spirit, of joints and of marrow,
and discerning the thoughts and intentions of the heart.

HEBREWS 4:12

One day, two guys started talking in a sporting goods store. They soon discovered they both owned the same rifle, a Winchester Model 94 level action. Both had owned their gun for fifty-plus years. The first guy said that he loved his rifle so much that he placed it above the mantel and never shot a round through it, and he often dusts it to keep it in tip-top shape. But it had never felt the crisp, cold air from the deer woods. The second guy said that he loved his gun so much that he never went into the woods without it. Over the years it had gotten some dents, dings, and scratches, and the finish was quite worn. There was even a little rust on the barrel. but it was the truest shooting gun he'd ever owned, and he had faith that it would never fail him in the moment of truth.

When it comes to the Word of God, do you just place it on the end table and dust it off every now and then? Or do you wield it like the doubled-edged, soul-piercing Excalibur that God has intended it to be?

Being raised in the church, I've witnessed a parenting style that has developed over the past several decades that is crippling our children. We raise our kids, telling them that

Jesus loves them and died for them, but we never actually train them in the Word of God and its power. They grow up to be biblically illiterate adults who are crushed under the weight of the world, because we neglected to give them a foundation rooted in the promises of God. So they began to doubt if Jesus really does love them.

If we give our children the sword but never teach them to use it, we send them to the frontlines of war destined for failure, and they'll be slaughtered by the darkness.

As I've said, the war does not discriminate. It seeks and consumes everyone who takes breath on this earth. Even Jesus was tested and tempted. As we read in Matthew 4, he thwarted the devil's attacks by reciting the truth of Scripture. We read there that this temptation from the devil came after Jesus was led into the wilderness, where the devil's third attack there went like this:

> Again, the devil took him to a very high mountain and showed him all the kingdoms of the world and their glory. And he said to him, "All these I will give you, if you will fall down and worship me." Then Jesus said to him, "Be gone, Satan! For it is written, 'You shall worship the Lord your God and him only shall you serve.'" Then the devil left him, and angels came and attended him. (Matthew 4:810)

God has provided us with everything we need to claim victory in our war. Like the two men talking in the sporting goods store, one chose to hang his gun on display, often dusting it to keep it pristine. The other man, however, chose to use it for what it was designed for. He used it until it was worn out, and instead of having a gun on the mantel to show-off, he had a house filled with stories, each with a unique testimony allowing him an opportunity to share.

Unless we train our children with the weapons the Lord has given, our kids become useless in defeating the devil. We must immerse our children in God's Word. Read it to them, memorize it with them, and pray it over them. Raise them to walk through this world with the love of Jesus in their mouth and the sword of truth in their hand.

The Bible shouldn't become another item to just dust off, but rather a weapon that will provide evidence of a Christ-driven warrior that has grown within. I don't write this from a place of wisdom as father, but as living proof as a son that the intentional and deliberate actions of a father to teach, speak of, and live out the truths of Scripture hold weight in a child's life. Our kids may act like they don't care or aren't listening, and it will drive you mad. This is where the devil will do his best to make you feel like your efforts are in vain. Whatever you do, don't give up teaching your children Scripture and its importance in their lives— because it matters. And they're listening, I promise.

As Theodore Roosevelt famously said, "Speak softly and carry a big stick."

THE ARMORY

Proverbs 20:7

2 Timothy 3:15-16

13

THE ARMOR OF A WARRIOR

Let me hear in the morning of your steadfast love,
for in you I trust.
Make me know the way I should go,
for to you I lift up my soul.

PSALM 143:8

It's difficult for fathers to fathom the power and influence we have over our children and their lives. We've been entrusted with their lives. God has ordained us to show them the way they should walk. They take their first breath dependent on our leadership, and they wake up daily relying on us to be who God created us to be.

Through your words you can build confidence or create resentment. Through your actions you can build leaders or create children who have no foundation and will be beaten down by the world. Are we using this influence to build them up or tear them down?

The truth is, stagnant, passive, uninvolved fathering is just as harmful to the physical and spiritual maturing of our kids as an absent father. The world is harsh and unforgiving, and a father's love is the armor that allows them to wage their war.

It has been said that there's nothing more powerful than a father's love. That power can have a positive or negative impact, depending on how we choose to utilize it. One of the greatest impacts a father's love has is how it molds our children's view of God their heavenly Father, and of his love for them and interaction with them. Our love, or lack thereof, literally forms the lens our children see God through. If a child cannot feel loved by their earthly dad or depend on that love, how can we expect them to comprehend the love of God?

The greatest example we have of how to love our wives, children, and community around us is how God himself loves us. We're to do our best to apply this example to our own lives. God's love for us is unconditional and widespread. We see God's love for us through his provision for us. He also loves us through his protection, through his intentionality, through his affirmation, and through his love for the world around us.

You may say, "I love my kids in my own way," or, "They know I love them; I don't have to tell them." But I come back at you with this: If you call yourself a Christian and you claim to have Christ in you, then you're a new creation in Christ and are called to take off the old and put on the new. This means you begin to be molded into the likeness of Christ. Therefore, we're to love like Christ in *all* these categories. Checkmate!

So—are we loving as God does? Stay tuned to find out!

1 John 4:16

Ephesians 5:25-26

Colossians 3:14

2 Thessalonians 3:5

14

LOVE THROUGH PROVISION

*Abraham lifted up his eyes and looked, and behold, behind him was a ram,
caught in a thicket by his horns. And Abraham went and took the ram
and offered it up as a burnt offering instead of his son.
So Abraham called the name of that place, "The LORD will provide";
as it is said to this day, "On the mount of the LORD it shall be provided."*

GENESIS 22:13-14

God's love is deep and wide. There's literally no facet of our lives that his love doesn't touch.

One of the most tangible ways we can feel God's love is through his provision for us. He's a God who provides. We see this over and over in the Scriptures—as when Jesus feeds five thousand people in Luke 9, or in Genesis 22 when a ram is provided by God for Abraham's sacrifice, in place of his son Isaac. I guarantee that you can see this loving provision in your own life as well.

God wants what's best for his children. He supplies our needs, but our sin has caused us to have jealously and envy. That in turn causes us to feel as if we're not loved, because the neighbors have a newer house or a newer vehicle or whatever. We want what they have, and we wonder why God doesn't provide it.

We must first understand that God's loving provision is perfect. He gives us exactly what we need when we need it. And if we have that perspective when he decides to give a bit more than our expectations, we find ourselves filled with gratitude rather than entitlement.

Jesus speaks on God's provision for us in these words: "Look at the birds of the air: they neither sow nor reap nor gather into barns, and yet your heavenly Father feeds them. Are you not of more value than they?" (Matthew 6:26).

As fathers, are we providing for our children? Honestly, I think this is the easiest responsibility for us as men to fulfill. We're hard-wired that way. It's in our DNA. There's nothing more satisfying for me than watching my kids sleep peacefully in a house that I worked to provide, or to eat a meal around a table I worked to supply.

One reason I love hunting and fishing so much is the provisional pride I get when I kill a deer or catch a fish and process it myself, cook it on the grill, and then watch my family partake and enjoy the fruits of my labor. We get joy from seeing others enjoying what we provided.

The downfall is when that deceiver Satan draws us in, and we get stuck in the trap of excess. We begin to see what others have and we want the same, but that requires more work, which requires us to be less present in the lives of our family. When we fall into this trap, we unfortunately take the most important thing we can provide for our kids and try to replace it with material things of the world, which aren't capable of filling the hole we created.

Our time and attention are the greatest things we can provide for our children to help them grow spiritually and physically. The newest clothes, newest house, latest gaming console, newest phone—all this means nothing if our kids are destined to hell because we replaced our provision of the spiritual side of life with material things of this world. We're called to be spiritual providers to our wives and children.

We can't do that if we're never physically present, when we're always off trying to provide only the things of this world.

A while back, I spent some time with a church and their staff. One of their core values was "excellence without excess." Get what you need to get the job done with excellence, but don't venture into the game of excess and wanting the newest and shiniest things. As I spent the week with them, I heard that quote from top to bottom; from lead pastor to volunteer and everyone in between, it was engrained in their culture. As my time with that church came to an end, I asked one of the staff members why they had that as a core value, and she said, "Because if you are always reaching for the excess you begin to lose focus on the purpose of the church—the people."

Here's the cold hard truth: If we lose sight of our people—our family—because we're concentrating more on the excess of provision, then we're failures in the fight against the enemy. If the devil can't make you bad, he'll make you busy.

THE ARMORY

Philippians 4:19
Psalm 37:25-26
John 10:10

15

LOVE THROUGH PROTECTION

You are a hiding place for me; you preserve me from trouble;
you surround me with shouts of deliverance.

PSALM 32:7

Am I safe? That's a question every person instinctively asks. They may not verbalize it, but deep in their soul they want to feel safe and protected. This is why we have a culture obsessed with superheroes. We want to know that no matter what comes into our city, we have someone who's going to fight for us and dispel the evil that lurks outside our door.

As believers in Jesus Christ, we've been given a promise that almighty God, the creator of the universe, will protect us. This promise is repeated over and over in Scripture. (Check the "Armory" at this chapter's end for a few references.)

God watches over us out of love, not out of obligation. The same should be said of us as fathers, as we shield our wives and children from the advances of the enemy.

I feel like this is another slam dunk in the category of fathers showing love. I think we instinctively want to protect our families. It's not something that's taught; it's bred into our God-given genetics. I've thought many times about what I would do if someone broke into my house and posed a threat to my family. Some may say you should share the gospel; I agree with you, though I'd probably prefer to share Jesus as the EMTs are hauling the intruder out the door, or as Saint Peter is penciling him in for an appointment at the pearly gates.

In the movie *Man on Fire* with Denzel Washington, there's a scene where his character is tracking down kidnappers who have a young girl that he was sworn to protect. He's hunting the kidnappers, and a man tells Denzel, "In the church, they say to forgive." Denzel responds with "Forgiveness is between them and God; it's my job to arrange the meeting."

This is and will always be my approach if you decide to come into my house uninvited with intent to harm or put my family at risk. I will protect, with my life, what God has placed under my charge. I pray all men have that fire in their soul.

But one thing we must not forget is that we're protectors not only in the physical realm, but also in the spiritual. If we truly love our children and want to protect them, we need to safeguard their soul from intrusions of the devil. Just as you would protect them from an intruder in your home, you need to fortify the spiritual house of their soul.

Unfortunately, we as parents in the church have failed at this over the past three decades, and the proof is in the massive amount of young adults who are being rebaptized because they admit they didn't know what it truly meant to follow Christ.

I see two deficient styles of parenting that are equally deadly to the spiritual health of our children. The first is that of parents who attend church but allow their kids complete freedom to attend or participate in church as they desire. What I find sad is that the majority of parents in this category have stricter expectations on the child's schooling than they do of the child's learning and absorbing God's Word. These kids never understand the importance of the body of Christ, and they get swallowed up by the world, selling their soul without ever realizing what they've done.

The second category includes parents who are all in and really care for the spiritual health and well-being of their child. Every time the doors are open, they're in the church. Their kids serve and participate—but they're also bubble-wrapped. All they know is the comfort of the church, and for eighteen years they're sheltered from the evil realities of the world. How is one supposed to step onto the battlefield of spiritual war when all they've known is a picture of Jesus in a green meadow with a lamb on his lap? Jesus of the Bible is not a soft, go-with-the-flow, kumbaya type. Jesus of the Bible drives out demons, he heals the sick, and he flips tables out of righteous anger. The heavens worship him, the wind and the waves listen to him, and when he offers his name as the great I Am, armies fell to the ground in trembling fear.

If we don't raise our kids to know the truth of the world firsthand, our children will turn out to be either self-righteous pricks, or soft and weak disciples who fold under the tiniest amount of pressure from the devil. They'll spend their life hugging the balance beam and avoiding the world, missing out on opportunities to rescue souls.

Our children of course will one day be adults, so we must train them to extinguish the fiery arrows of the devil. We need to train our children for war, which means exposing them little by little to the reality of the world and allowing them to utilize their faith as we guide them through situations. Allow them to experience their faith for what it truly is, and not as just words in a book. Sharpen their skills so that when you release them into this world, they're well equipped and confident in their faith and can walk into the darkness with the light of Christ and win souls for his kingdom.

A kid can sit in a classroom for three weeks learning how to swim, but until they get in the pool, all that knowledge means nothing.

THE ARMORY

Psalm 121:7-8

Isaiah 43:2

Proverbs 18:10-12

2 Timothy 4:18-20

2 Thessalonians 3:3-5

16

LOVE THROUGH AFFIRMATION

And a voice from heaven said,
"This is my Son, whom I love;
with him I am well pleased."

MATTHEW 3:17 NIV

One of the most underrated tools we have as a father is our words. Our words possess the power to build or destroy the hearts of our children.

As men, we often get hardened and passive about affirming our children. Being silent with words of affirmation is not biblical, nor is it manly, nor is it godly. Affirmation from a father is the fuel that ignites the souls of our children to climb mountains, make new discoveries, and run full speed into the darkest corners of the world in order to shine the light of truth and bring hope to a broken world. Deep in our souls, every single person is yearning for their father to say, "This is my child, whom I love, who I'm well pleased with."

As a dad, my job is to know my children and help them discover God's purpose in their life. I then build them up and steward them into that purpose.

One of the greatest questions we can ask our kids is "What are you passionate about?" The world does not need more nine-to-fivers; it needs young men and women pursuing their passions and making much of the gospel of Christ through those passions.

I can remember my dad sitting down with my wife and me early in our marriage, as we discussed pursuing a life of ministry by starting our own nonprofit ministry focused on fatherhood. My dad told me, "In this life you have to decide: Do you want to pursue making money or pursue building this idea?" My wife and I looked at each other and exclaimed that we wanted to pursue ministry, since that's where our passion lay. My dad warned us to be ready to work harder than ever and be prepared to give up the expectations of the world. Then he asked how he could help! After my dad gave us perspective on what to expect, he said, "I'm behind you a hundred percent." He gave us the courage to step out.

Has pursuing this ministry been hard? Extremely. Have there been tears? Absolutely. Will there be more? Without a doubt. But we're fervently pursuing what God has called us to. We're pursuing it with passion.

Our children will look to us for guidance and confirmation in their lives. Don't squelch their passions because you think they're unattainable. If they're pursuing God and deepening their faith in him, then let them run as far as they can in pursuit of Christ and his calling on their life. Constantly tell them you love them and are proud of them, and ask how you can support them in their passions. Every word of affirmation you pour over them will fill their soul more and more with the courage it will take to wage their war in this life.

Our words are what they'll hold on to once we're gone. It's what sustains them and allows them to stand tall and confident in the face of the certain adversity this world will bring to their doorstep. Have you done everything you can to prepare them?

2 Timothy 1:7

1 Timothy 3:2

LOVE THROUGH INTENTIONALITY

*O LORD, you have searched me
and known me!*

PSALM 139:1

father is charged with the responsibility to raise and disciple his children. We're called to be the spiritual leaders in our homes, and God has ordained us as the primary source of spiritual guidance and instruction in the lives of our kids. We must stand firm and stay alert, because the devil will lull us to sleep and cause us to get passive in the pursuit of the spiritual growth of our children.

What it takes is intentionality. We must pursue our kids and their hearts daily. To make a difference in a life, we must first invest in that life. That means intentionally getting to know who they are and how God has crafted them. Every child has been fearfully and wonderfully made, and God has gifted them individually with talents and strengths to walk through life giving glory to the name of Jesus. The job of a father is to steward his children and help them refine and sharpen those skills so they can fulfill their purpose and be warriors in the kingdom of Christ. One of the simplest ways we can do this is by asking questions and intently listening to the answers, allowing our children to vocalize who they are.

One thing I started with my daughter when she was around three was a game called Four Questions. I ask her four questions of any kind, then she asks me four. What's your favorite color? What's your favorite food? Do you like being outside or inside? Dress or jeans? Princess or superhero?

While these questions feel superficial and insignificant, what I'm doing is getting to know who she is and also creating a space where she's comfortable asking her dad questions, and in turn me asking her questions. I'm building trust in her heart that I'm here for her and want the best for her, because one day the questions will not be so superficial, nor the topics so shallow. One day there will be questions that deal with the eternal resting place of her soul, and the devil will do whatever he can to distract her, shame her, and make her feel stupid to even ask. But she can come to me with confidence knowing that I'll listen and respond with love and truth that comes from the Word of God.

I was hosting a father-son hunting retreat a few years ago and had spoken with the dads about investing in their son's lives. I suggested that while they were in the deer stand, fathers could ask their sons some questions and just listen, without formulating a response. *Just listen.* We have a bad habit as adults with our kids of asking questions and then immediately rushing into correction mode.

That evening, I checked back in with the dads. One dad said that it started off well. He asked generic questions and conversation started. But the moment he asked a question with a little meat to it, the son looked at him and said, "Dad, what are you doing? Why are you being weird? We don't do this. You don't ever ask me about me." And the son shut down. The dad sat there in silence feeling defeated and realizing he'd never intentionally pursued his son. This dad had tears in his eyes as he spoke with me.

The longer we wait, the harder it becomes. And even if you start early, there will be hurdles to navigate. But if your child doesn't trust you to speak about things in their life—like school, relationships, or life choices—they'll never trust you to speak into their spiritual lives.

We must begin cultivating the soil of our children's hearts and souls from day one. If the ground is hard when there's planting to be done, the soil will not yield produce. If our children are only hearing about Jesus for one to two hours a week on Sunday and Wednesday, we're failing as fathers. If that statement offends you, good! It means the Holy Spirit is working on the dark corners of your own heart. It's time we step up and invest in our children and provide daily spiritual guidance and wisdom, raising them to be who God created them to be. To do this, we must take time to discover who they are, what they're passionate about, and how God has gifted them. Then we leverage that information to raise our kids in the purpose God created them for.

THE ARMORY

Acts 2:39

Ephesians 6:4

Galatians 6:1

18

LOVE THROUGH COMMUNITY

Where there is no guidance, a people falls,
but in an abundance of counselors there is safety.

PROVERBS 11:14

One of the greatest gifts my parents bestowed on me was allowing other godly men and women to have influence in my life. They strategically built a community around me that could pour truth into my soul. Even though we as fathers are called to be the main spiritual influence in our family, we also need to acknowledge that God has gifted others to make huge impacts in our kids' lives. We need to recognize those people and intentionally place them in the path of our children. These could be teachers, coaches, people at church, people in our social circles, or anyone we see as an asset in the building up of our children. We need to have conversations with these people and let them know our hearts and desires for our kids, and then ask if they would be willing to join us in fighting for the souls of our children. We're essentially commissioning them as spiritual bodyguards in our kids' lives, and we ask that they'll pray for them and find opportunity to speak wisdom and life-changing truth into their souls.

In my life, I've had many of these people who fought for me. As a kid I never really noticed their intentions, but now as an adult I'm eternally grateful for their hearts and their impact in my life. Some of these individuals were in my life for many years; with others, I had only a weekend. But they all served a purpose in directing me into the man I am today.

As a father I must provide love to my children through community. This is the picture of the body of Christ and as fathers we need to allow the arms of the body to wrap around our kids. My hope is that I provide my children with opportunities to experience the fullness of the body of Christ. I want them to rub shoulders with people who love Jesus, people from all races, countries, backgrounds, economic status, and denominations. I want them to experience God beyond the bubble of influence we have in our daily lives. I want them to know God deeper and to see him work beyond the limits of our little Baptist church in the middle of nowhere Georgia, where the demographic is extremely white. I want them to know the God of the universe, and the people he calls redeemed. And I want the body of Christ to know my children.

As Paul says, "So we, though many, are one body in Christ, and individually members one of another" (Romans 12:5).

THE ARMORY

Hebrews 10:24-25

Galatians 6:2

Matthew 18:20

1 John 1:7

19

QUIET CONFIDENCE

He has told you, O man, what is good;
and what does the LORD require of you
but to do justice, and to love kindness,
and to walk humbly with your God?

MICAH 6:8

Humility is lacking in our culture today, and unfortunately it's hard to find even inside the walls of the church and its leadership. A large majority of pastors, preachers, ministry leaders, and influencers of the faith have built the platforms they stand on around their own identity. They use the gospel as a tool for popularity, notoriety, financial gain, and status. They've allowed pride to take control. As fathers, we're called to be the pastor, preacher, ministry leader, and main influencers in the church we call home.

My question to you is this: Are you walking humbly with your God? Are you showing your children what it means to live a life of humility under the lordship of Jesus Christ?

If we want to raise our children to be warriors for the kingdom, they must first understand that every hedge of protection, every blessing, and every victory comes directly from God and is nothing of our own doing. Are we teaching that to our kids? To walk humbly with our God means that we daily live out these words spoken by John the Baptist about Jesus: "He must increase, but I must decrease" (John

3:30). Are we teaching our children to deflect the praise given to us and direct it back to God?

I played baseball growing up. My sophomore year of high school, I had the best game of my career. I went four for four, with three triples and a single. Right before my last at bat, my assistant coach approached me while I was on deck. He said, "Whether in baseball or in life, a real man steps forward with quiet confidence. He knows and is confident in his ability, but is humble enough to brag only on the One who gave him his ability."

I've tried to live my life in that humility ever since. All glory and honor goes back to Christ, the author and perfecter of my faith.

If we fail to raise our kids to understand and walk in humility, then pride begins to fester, and our kids become self-righteous pricks who build walls and create divisions that separate others from the love of Christ. Sound familiar? Kind of looks like the church in America, does it not?

Humility is not an attribute we readily teach in our culture; we see humility as weakness. As men, we see it as unmanly. And yet we read in Philippians 2:8 that Jesus humbled himself in obedience to God, even to the point of dying a criminal's death. When we walk in humility, our humility shines the power of Christ to the world around us. In our humility, others can see that our lives are not about us but all about Christ, who decided to humble himself and die for you and me even when we were still sinners. A strong warrior in Christ knows the source of their ability and power, and walks daily in that humility.

Paul said it best, in words we looked at earlier. After Jesus told him, "My grace is sufficient for you, for my power is made perfect in weakness," Paul declared, "Therefore, I will boast all the more gladly of my weaknesses, so that the power of Christ may rest upon me" (2 Corinthians 12:9)

As men, husbands, and fathers, we must stay humble in the raising of our children, knowing that the moment we let pride in the door, we've lost all control. Pride is the noose that suffocates the Great Commission; humility is the cross that brings salvation to all mankind. Pick up your cross every day, and follow Jesus.

THE ARMORY

Proverbs 3:26

Isaiah 41:10

2 Corinthians 3:5

Philippians 4:13

20

THE WEAPON OF WISDOM

The wisdom that comes from heaven is first of all pure;
then peace-loving, considerate, submissive,
full of mercy and good fruit, impartial and sincere.

JAMES 3:17 NIV

In the age of smart phones, social media, and instant notifications, we've thrown away one of the greatest weapons we can possess as a warrior in kingdom of Christ. That weapon is *wisdom*.

Wisdom is woven into the fibers of Scripture. The book of Proverbs is devoted solely to the topic of wisdom. As followers of Christ, we're called to be filled with wisdom, and if we lack it, then we should ask our heavenly Father to provide it to us.

One of the devil's greatest tactics is to distract us. He loves to preoccupy us with battles that have no eternal significance and do nothing but tire us out and cause us to build walls that separate others from hearing about Jesus.

You may have heard the saying, "Is that a hill worth dying on?" This is a question we need to ask at every point of conflict. We must keep the main thing the main thing, and that thing is Jesus. The church today has chosen to get distracted by small insignificant battles (some internal and some external) that accomplish nothing and unfortunately stunt the growth of the gospel into the nations of the world.

As we raise our children, we need to allow them the privilege of exercising their wisdom. We often think wisdom is a gift granted only to a few, but it's more of a muscle we all need to strengthen. Wisdom is made up of two parts: the truths of Scripture, and its application in a real-world scenario. If you don't know the Scriptures, you cannot be wise in the spiritual realms, and if you never apply those truths, then you'll never gain wisdom.

As I raise my kids, I will speak about and pray over the truths written on the pages of Scripture; I'll live out these truths and walk my kids through them. I will immerse their lives with the promises of God. Then I'll actively and intentionally look for opportunities that allow my children to apply God's Word in their day-to-day life, through conversations, interactions, decisions, and conflicts. Will they make mistakes? Absolutely! You cannot learn to ride a bike without a scraped knee or two. But no matter what, I'll be right beside them to pick them up, dust them off, and help them get back on the bike.

The devil wants you to believe that Scripture knowledge is good enough. But knowledge without application is foolishness. True wisdom is the application of the gospel in the forward movement of Christ. We must train our kids to ask, "Is what I'm about to say or do going to bring others toward Jesus or push them away? Am I building the kingdom of Christ or tearing its walls down?"

The devil will use the world and its shortcomings to try and trap us away from graciously proclaiming the kingdom of Christ, as well as being grateful for it. "Let us be grateful for receiving a kingdom that cannot be shaken" (Hebrews

12:28). Wisdom stands firm on the foundational truth that the kingdom of God is unshakeable, so our job is not to defend his kingdom, but to go out in rescue missions to bring others into his kingdom.

And take note: "A fool takes no pleasure in understanding, but only in expressing his opinion" (Proverbs 18:2); "Even a fool who keeps silent is considered wise; when he closes his lips, he is deemed intelligent" (Proverbs 17:28). Often the wisest thing we can do is to stand quietly—not expressing our personal opinions—and by doing so we extinguish the obstacles of the devil.

The devil will use the world to try and trap you into playing his game and make you feel that you're fighting for a just cause. Wisdom is the shield in which we deflect the fiery arrows of the enemy that aim to distract us from the real fight. Our fight is to point others to Jesus. Everything else is a distraction.

THE ARMORY

James 1:5

James 3:17

Proverbs 3:13-18

21

A WARRIOR NEEDS COMPASSION

Jesus said, "Father, forgive them,
for they do not know what they are doing."

LUKE 23:34

Compassion is one of the attributes of God, yet men have the hardest time with understanding compassion and providing it to their families and communities. We often think of compassion as a feminine character trait. We feel that fathers should be strong, stoic, and steadfast, while mothers are nurturing, loving, and compassionate.

I see this in my own life. When one of my kids is crying from getting hurt doing something that I've told them a hundred times not to do, my general response is, "When you play stupid games, you win stupid prizes."

When I actually take time to think it over, I'm really glad God doesn't treat me in that manner. I mess up daily in such a way that God could look down, shaking his finger and reminding me, "If you weren't so stupid..."

Instead he sent his Son Jesus, and in the most compassionate act in world history, Jesus was beaten, mocked, shamed, spit upon, and nailed to the cross because of what we did. Through it all, Jesus still had the compassion to cry out to God on our behalf and say, "Father, forgive them, for they do not know what they are doing." He had the compassion to take on himself the beating and suffering that I deserve, and in the midst of the pain and agony he still pleaded to God on my behalf—so that now when I mess up, God looks down and Jesus says, "I covered that!"

So my question for you is this: Are we as fathers showing and teaching our children compassion? If the creator of the universe in his indisputable perfection and sovereignty can find compassion in his heart to rescue this wretched soul from the depths of eternal suffering that is much deserved, then I think as men we need to embrace compassion—not just as a manly attribute, but moreover a godly one.

If we call ourselves the body of Christ but we lack that compassion in our hearts that gave us the eternal life our faith is built on, then do we really have the salvation we claim? Our hearts should be burdened for what God is burdened for.

We're called image bearers of Christ—what reflection do our kids see when they see our lives in action? Again I'll say this: Our children won't do what we tell them; they'll do what we *show* them. Are we showing them compassion? The compassion of a warrior in the kingdom of Christ should be like butter in my grandmother's kitchen: on everything!

Ephesians 4:32

Mark 6:34

Colossians 3:12-13

2 Corinthians 1:3-4

22

A WARRIOR NEEDS CONVICTION

Stand therefore, having fastened on the belt of truth,
and having put on the breastplate of righteousness.

EPHESIANS 6:14

Every night I pray over my children. One of my requests to God is that he gives them a spirit of conviction to stand firm on the truths of his Word. I pray that their lives are so rooted in the promises of God that they'll stand firm, unwavering in the face of persecution, even if that means standing alone, and even if it means losing their life.

In our current western culture of lukewarm Christians and the ever growing prosperity, I see a big issue of people claiming the name of Christ, but under pressure from the culture they either fade away or begin to use culture to drive changes to the gospel. One thing that we need to understand is that *the gospel never changes*! When we begin to misuse Scripture to justify or normalize our actions in regard to culture and social spectrums, we're playing a dangerous game that has eternal consequences.

Just know this: God will not be mocked, and he has the final word. We're either with him or against him. You're saved from his judgment and wrath only because of the spilt blood of Jesus on the cross. If you remove that foundational truth, everything built on top crumbles.

As I raise my kids, I'm not raising them to blend into culture; I'm raising them to change culture. I'm not raising them to go with the flow; I'm raising them to redirect the flow directly to the feet of Jesus. I want them to be world-changers, and they must have enough conviction to withstand the pressure of an ungodly culture that's growing in strength through every passing generation.

I want my kids to live a life worthy of the gospel of Christ, and if they do, they best believe that the devil is going to wage war against them. A warrior with no conviction cowers and hides at the sound of the first cannon blast. I pray that I'm raising my kids to stand firm, to build their life on a solid foundation of God's Word. And though they may get beaten and bruised by this world, they never stop reaching out to pull others from the flood waters that would sweep them away, and to plant these others safely on solid ground.

The devil will tell you that knowledge of the gospel is good enough. I don't want my kids to just know the gospel, I want them to *live* the gospel. Knowledge without conviction is madness. Knowledge of Scripture without conviction to do what it says is like reading a sign that says, "Swim at own risk—infested with alligators," then tying chickens to your waist and jumping in. Unfortunately, people in the church are lining up to go swimming, and culture is standing at the water's edge selling chickens at half price. Although we know we shouldn't buy the chickens, there's something tempting about them. We in the church are failing to teach our kids how to live the gospel, and in doing so we're condemning generation after generation to eternal damnation.

So the question becomes: How do we instill conviction into the hearts of our children? To be blunt, this is impossible without introducing them to the Holy Spirit. Apart from the Holy Spirit's work, there's nothing we as fathers can do to cultivate a heart of conviction in our children. Therefore we must plead with God to make himself known to them. We must intercede on our children's behalf by praying for their soul, praying for the mercy and grace that they don't yet know they need. And we must take advantage of every opportunity to introduce them to the Spirit of God.

The greatest way we can do this is by the life we live in front of them. Just as Jesus said: "Truly, truly, I say to you, the Son can do nothing of his own accord, but only what he sees the Father doing. For whatever the Father does, that the Son does likewise" (John 5:19).

If the Spirit lives in us, then every moment is an opportunity to make an introduction that has life-changing purpose in the eternal continuum.

THE ARMORY

John 16:8

Titus 1:9

Romans 2:15

23

EVERY WARRIOR IS UNIQUE

For as in one body we have many members,
and the members do not all have the same function,
so we, though many, are one body in Christ,
and individually members one of another.

ROMANS 12:4-5

Raising your children is one of the most challenging things you will do. Each child is uniquely created by God, and because of that, each one requires special attention that's unique to their soul. Not every kid is motivated, encouraged, disciplined, or discipled in the same way. Our job as fathers is to know our children intimately so that we can effectively guide them through life.

One of my past coaches told me that a great coach discovers each player's strengths and weaknesses, and uses each player accordingly. You cannot expect a Corvette to do the same job as a dump truck, and vice versa. If you drive every player the same, both you and the player will grow in frustration, and in the long run you'll lose the game that's before you.

When it comes to your kids, are you individually investing in who God created them to be? Or are you driving them all the same? One of my greatest joys is discovering who my kids are and seeing their individual personalities flourish. My oldest daughter is a social butterfly who loves meeting new people, has a big heart for hospitality, and is a rule follower. She's also very sensitive, and her feelings are easily hurt.

My son is shy and reserved in crowds, but when you crack through the shy exterior, he's a goofball who loves making people laugh. He's also hardheaded and determined. He's a kid who pushes back to see just how much he can get away with. As I write this, my wife and I are expecting another daughter, and we pray diligently for her and the woman that God has created her to be. Ultimately, how I engage and motivate my children will look quite different for each one, but the life I live in front of them should always point them back to Jesus.

I tell fathers all the time, "Your kids will never do what you tell them; they'll do what you do." My character, my convictions, how I handle relationships, and how I love their mother has greater impact on who they become than my words ever could.

One day, young men will be knocking on my door to ask me for my daughter's hand in marriage. How I live my life in front of my daughters will have a direct reflection in the men they find to marry. I pray these men are godly men, and so I pray that I am a godly man. I pray that my daughters grow up having character and integrity, finding their worth in what their heavenly Father says about them as royalty in his court. For my son, I want him to know what it truly means to lead and love like Jesus. I want him to see my words in action, and I want him to take up the charge of a man of the Lord, so he can lead with courage and conviction as he protects those who've been placed under his care, and provides for them physically and spiritually. If this is my desire for all my children, I must daily find ways to individually build them into the image of Christ. There are no cookie cutter kids in the body of Christ.

Our natural bent is to raise our kids through supervision. We want to tell them what to do and then correct them when they mess up. But a true father raises his children as a guide. He's out front in the world with them, walking with them, showing them, and often encouraging them and pushing them to step out of their comfort zone to create growth in their lives, knowing that failure creates perseverance and courage to face life when they're eventually released into this world on their own.

Dads, drop the "I told you so," and pick up the "Let me show you." For this is what Jesus did for us when he humbled himself and took human form and walked this life with us. God intentionally and uniquely crafted the inner being of your child for great purpose in the building of the kingdom of Christ. And we are tasked with the responsibility of helping each child discover that purpose, and stewarding them in their uniqueness for the glory of God.

It's time we get to work!

Psalm 139:13-14

1 Peter 2:9

24

TESTED BY FIRE

These trials will show that your faith is genuine.
It is being tested as fire tests and purifies gold—
though your faith is far more precious than mere gold.
So when your faith remains strong through many trials,
it will bring you much praise and glory and honor
on the day when Jesus Christ is revealed to the whole world.

1 PETER 1:7 NLT

One of my greatest fears is that one day my kids will stand before the throne of God and be told by the creator of the universe, "I never knew you; depart from me" (Matthew 7:23).

One of the greatest deceptions in the twenty-first-century church is the lie that well-behaved, church-attending kids are secure in the salvation of the Lord. I don't care if they have all the right "church" answers to our "church" questions, if their answers aren't deeply rooted in their heart, and if the truth hasn't transformed the inner being of who they are, it's merely lip service to the gospel of Christ.

It's up to us to test the hearts of our children and to dive into the core of who they are, to see that their faith is genuine. This is a difficult process for most fathers. It requires that we put our kids in situations that will cause them to put into action the words they hear or speak on a Sunday morning. It requires intentional intimacy with our children. We essentially throw them in the fire and allow them to wrestle with the faith they claim to have. This will often result in failure and some amount of heartache. But we're always standing on the other side with open arms to love, encourage, and give guidance.

In I Peter 1:7, we see our faith compared to gold being tested and purified. A goldsmith takes raw gold and sets it into the fire to remove and burn away all the impurities that have been infused into it after years of being buried in the earth. The same is true for our faith. We've been infused by impurities of sin, misguided culture, and our own misconceptions of God and what he has called us to do. As fathers, we're called to act as goldsmiths for our kids, and one of the greatest things we can do for them is to place them in the fire so the impurities of this world can be burned away.

Unfortunately, the vast majority of parents in the church today are ignorant about the state of their child's heart. They seem to have little or no interest in investing in and testing the faith of their child. Instead, what we've created and taught in the church culture today is to just place our child in a Christian bubble in all aspects of life. The issue with that mindset is that it completely eliminates the call of the Great Commission in the lives of our children. How can they go if we've always taught them to stay? In my opinion, this is a huge factor in the mass decline of the western church. For decades, we sat still and expected others to step into our bubble, while the Great Commission calls us to go out to others in the world and engage them in *their* bubble. We've stepped away from God's plan while becoming comfortable in our own plan.

Let's change the tide. Let's start raising generations of young men and women who will pick up the call to go into this world, and who will not just sit, soak and sour in the faith that was meant to change the world.

1 Peter 5:10

Psalm 34:19

25

A WARRIOR NEEDS TO BE RELEASED

*Like arrows in the hands of a warrior
are children born in one's youth.*

PSALM 127:4

ow I see my children has direct influence on how I parent, so it's vitally important that I see them in the way that God sees them. Scripture likens our children to arrows. This arrow image offers significant insight on how we raise our children. If you aren't familiar with archery, let me explain the visual King David is trying to get across.

In ancient times, and still today, archers are a very exacting group. They test, tune, and perfect their equipment meticulously. They do everything they can to ensure that their arrow hits its mark. Interestingly enough, the term *sin* is an archery term meaning "to miss the mark." Archers also spend countless hours tuning each individual arrow, because even in our technology-driven world today, it's impossible to create a perfectly straight arrow. The process of "nock tuning" is to discover the weak side and strong side of the arrow shaft and then adjusting the nock on the arrow to allow the veins (feathers) to spin the arrow in the air—creating balance among the strong and weak side of the arrow, so that the force from the bow is directed toward the target and not to the left or right. An archer will tune each arrow so that each one strikes the desired mark.

King David is telling us that each kid is unique with strengths and weaknesses. Sound familiar? But let me pose this question: What good is it if we have a perfectly tuned arrow, but don't allow it to be used as it was designed?

An arrow may sit in the quiver for a time, but it is designed ultimately to be released into the world, being led by a razor-sharp broadhead in order to inflict deep, soul-penetrating wounds. Every step of the process in raising our children leads to this moment in time. If we fail to release our children into the world fully prepared to make life-changing impact for the kingdom of Christ, our work is in vain.

An arrow can be released only by its archer. Any attempt to fly on its own will be unsuccessful. God has ordained fathers with the spiritual power to draw the bow that projects our children into flight with purpose and power.

May we release our arrows aimed directly at the heart of our world, being led by the razor-sharp Word of God—so that generations after generations will be reclaimed to the eternal kingdom of Christ.

Exodus 14:13–14

Deuteronomy 1:30–31

26

DANGEROUS PRAYERS

Behold, I am sending you out as sheep in the midst of wolves,
so be wise as serpents and innocent as doves. Beware of men,
for they will deliver you over to courts and flog you in their synagogues,
and you will be dragged before governors and kings for my sake,
to bear witness before them and the Gentiles.

MATTHEW 10:16-18

'm going to ask you to do something that will go against every fiber of your being as a father. I'm going to ask you to start praying dangerous prayers for your children that will most certainly put them in harm's way.

If we truly want to fight against the satanic powers of this world, then our job—our God-ordained responsibility—is to train our children to become warriors, and then push them to the frontlines of battle fully prepared to wage war on behalf of Christ's kingdom. We don't want kids who are only morally good, and who become culturally driven churchgoers while still theologically bankrupt. We want battle-ready warriors who walk through this world dispelling the darkness, protecting the weak, and rescuing the lost out of the pit of despair by sharing the life-changing news of the gospel. We want biblically sound, Jesus-following Christians—like the ones we read about in the book of Acts, who set the world on fire after being baptized in the Holy Spirit.

Raising up such as these is what God has called us to as fathers. This is what Jesus got nailed to the cross for.

We in the western church have a hard time wrapping our heads around this, but claiming the name of Christ will cost you something in this life on earth. Don't believe me? Read the book of Acts, or better yet talk with a Christ follower in places where they're persecuted, especially in various parts of Asia and Africa. These people proclaim Christ in baptism, and their life expectancy drops to mere days. Yet the church is still growing like wildfire in those countries. Our brothers and sisters abroad are living examples of these words for us from Paul: "To me, living means living for Christ, and dying is even better" (Philippians 1:21 NLT).

To the American believer, the tides are shifting. There will come a time when following Christ will truly cost you something. Are we preparing our children to be battle ready? Or will the tide of culture sweep them off their feet?

We've seen much opposition and persecution to Christians abroad, and many of these issues are showing up here in America. We often feel as Christians that we deserve better treatment, but don't be fooled! We're entering a time when it's going to cost you something to claim the name of Christ. It may be loss of a friendship or relationship, loss of a job or a family member, or maybe even your life—as we've seen on the news with the beheading of Christians overseas.

Yes, a time is coming when it will cost you something to claim Christ's name, and when that time comes, and you're brought before a judge and put on trial for being a follower of Jesus Christ—will there be enough evidence to convict you?

What does it mean to pray dangerous prayers for our children? It means praying that they pursue God's calling on their life with no boundaries or ultimatums. What does this tangibly look like? Here's my best example.

On a Sunday morning in 2018, I sat in church and listened to our pastor interview a mother who a few hours later would be putting her nineteen-year-old daughter on a plane to be a missionary in an undisclosed country. Even her mother had no idea where her daughter was going or where she would be. This young lady had spent the last few months preparing and training to engage people with the gospel of Christ in a hostile, life-threatening culture. She was entering a place where she could lose her life because of her faith. I vividly remember our pastor asking two specific questions to this mother:

"Why is your daughter doing this?"

"Tell me your feelings and thoughts."

The mother answered with tears in her eyes, but with perfect clarity: "My daughter is doing this because God has placed a burden and a calling on her life for these people, and as far as my feelings and thoughts, even though I have my fears, I pray that I can usher my daughter into her calling from the Lord because I would rather my daughter be obedient to the will of God and be in harm's way than be physically safe."

That's a dangerous prayer! God's will above all. Is this the prayer we have for our children?

If we truly want our kids to live for Christ, we must begin to pray that they'll be obedient to the will of the Lord, wherever it leads. We must pray dangerous prayers for our children and send them out as sheep among wolves.

If you've made it this far, you've made it to the starting line. Now let's start building our children in the truth of the gospel and raise them to be warriors. For God has ordained that our children are built by our hands, the hands of a warrior.

Then we need not fear the enemies of Christ. "Do not be afraid of them. Remember the LORD, who is great and awesome, and fight for your brothers, your sons, your daughters, your wives, and your homes" (Nehemiah 4:14).

Hebrews 4:16

Exodus 33:18

Hebrews 12:2

27

A WARRIOR'S HERITAGE

*He loved your fathers and chose their offspring after them
and brought you out of Egypt with his own presence, by his great power.*

DEUTERONOMY 4:37

When you look into the future and think about what you'll leave behind for your children when your life comes to an end, what comes to mind?

If you're like me, you're doing good just to keep your head above the water in the here and now, and thinking beyond next week is a struggle. But every so often in slow periods of my life, my mind wanders down those trails of the future, and I consider what I'm going to leave behind for my kids.

I think our minds naturally go to things that are tangible or materialistic, things we spent time building or acquiring. We think about money, houses, businesses, and vehicles. While these things are nice, I would boldly argue that the greatest thing we can pass on to our children is a strong biblical heritage. At the end of it all, how will great riches help us, our children, or our grandchildren in eternity? Plainly put: Not. One. Bit.

Mark 8:36 says, "For what does it profit a man to gain the whole world and forfeit his soul?" As we move forward in our pursuit of Christ, we need to acknowledge that our actions and our faith will have repercussions in future generations that we may never meet. The heritage of our faith—or lack thereof—will exist beyond our years on this earth.

To be clear, we must all individually work out our salvation by standing in reverent fear of God and surrendering our lives to his lordship. Just because I live a righteous life, my salvation is not counted toward my children. They must personally make a life-changing commitment to Christ. But through my life and a biblical heritage, I'm placing their feet on a solid foundation that has stood the test of the weight of the world. This is my story, the words of my testimony.

I grew up in the church, and I always thought my testimony was weak because I didn't have a powerful story of God rescuing me from a life of rebellion. I never thought my testimony could be useful to others. But as I grew older, I came to understand that my testimony points to what Moses told God's people long ago: "Because He loved your fathers, therefore He chose their descendants after them" (Deuteronomy 4:37 NKJV).

My testimony actually starts decades before I was born. My grandfather made a decision to follow Christ, and as a young married man he made it a priority to spiritually lead his wife and three sons. My dad was born in 1950 and was brought up in the church. He lived his life on his terms, but in the living room of a small parsonage, my dad surrendered his life to Christ. Because my grandfather had raised him in the truth of God's Word, my dad had a model to follow. My grandfather's life was a heritage that my father grasped on to and held tightly while he raised my sisters and me. Now that heritage is being passed on to his grandchildren.

My testimony has more to do with a man's decision from nearly sixty years prior to my birth than it does with my own choices. My grandad took our family tree, and in a mere moment of time began branching it toward the gospel of Jesus. I hope that one day his great-great-grandchildren will have the opportunity to hug him in heaven and thank him for the decision he made as a young man. This is the picture of biblical heritage. This is what it looks like to leave an eternal inheritance. The decisions you make about Christ today will forever impact the lives of those that will come after you.

So choose this day whom you will serve. "But as for me and my house, we will serve the LORD" (Joshua 24:15).

THE ARMORY

Psalm 127:3

Psalm 119:111

Deuteronomy 28:1-68

28

DIG DEEP WELLS

Blessed are those who hunger and thirst for righteousness,
for they shall be satisfied.

MATTHEW 5:6

Water is essential to life. The human body can survive only three days without it. Water is a top three of must haves in a survival situation. Plain and simple, without water we die.

Since the beginning of time, civilizations have been built around water. Living out in rural Georgia, my family relies on a well to serve our necessity for water. If my well shuts down, that means showers and toilets don't work, and there's no water to drink or cook with. When I bought the house, I had the well serviced, just for peace of mind. I asked the technician if the well's depth mattered, and he said, "The golden rule of wells is the deeper the better. The deeper you go, the higher the quality of water, and the less chance you run your well dry."

The question now becomes: Do we dig wells for the spiritual water that's essential for our souls? And how deep are we digging them?

Jesus once came to a well and talked there with a Samaritan woman, and he told her this: "Everyone who drinks of this water will be thirsty again, but whoever drinks the water I give them will never thirst. Indeed, the water I give them will become in them a spring of water welling up to eternal life" (John 4:13-14). Jesus was asserting that spiritual wells are more important than physical wells, and the well of Scripture brings eternal nourishment to our souls.

Growing up in the church and doing ministry over the years, I've come to realize that the vast majority of church goers and Christians are spiritually dry because they haven't immersed their lives in water from the well of Scripture. The Word of God is an unfathomably deep well that most people just skim the surface of. But remember, the deeper you go the better the quality.

The body of Christ, especially in the west, has become weak and lethargic. We're satisfied by sermons having minimal Scripture and tainted by personal opinions that lack ability to hydrate our souls. We need to reclaim our passion for Scripture, digging deep wells and then teaching our kids how to do the same, so that when the world dries up and our culture begins to suffer from a drought, we've dug wells that will never run dry. Then we can be a source of water for the thirsty to taste the redemptive love of Christ.

1 Corinthians 2:9-12

Exodus 33:18–34:9

29

ONE THOUSAND GENERATIONS

You shall not bow down to them or serve them,
for I the LORD your God am a jealous God,
visiting the iniquity of the fathers on the children
to the third and the fourth generation of those who hate me,
but showing steadfast love to thousands
of those who love me and keep my commandments.

EXODUS 20:5-6

How will I be remembered? What will my legacy be? Does my life make a difference?

These are questions I believe all men can contemplate in the back corners of our mind. The irony is that our legacy has more to do with those who come after us than it does with us individually.

I like this quote attributed to mixed martial artist and UFC champion Vitor Belfort: "Legacy is not what I did for myself. It is what I am doing for the next generation."

Are we living our lives in constant pursuit of Christ and making decisions that build solid foundations for the generations who will walk in our footsteps? As spiritual leaders, we're tasked with laying the foundation that our children will one day build their lives upon. Is that foundation cemented in the truth of God's Word? Are we taking the time and putting forth the effort to dig deep footers into the souls of our children, so their lives won't crumble under the weight of the world? Are we building legacies that will last for a thousand generations?

This is the hard work, the unseen work. Foundations of houses are underground, covered with dirt, and unseen to the general public. The same goes for the foundational work we do in the lives of our children. Strong foundations are built in our homes, around dinner tables, through intentional conversations, in how we love our wives, and in the godly character we visibly live out before our kids. We must show them that our faith actually means something to us—that it has actually changed us and defines the core of who we are. It should be the forefront of everything in our lives.

If we're faithful to do the work God has ordained for us as spiritual leaders, the legacy we build will reach souls for the kingdom of Christ for a millennia. Let's stay focused and determined in the task before us day by day, intentionally working to build our children up on the rock-solid foundation of God's Holy Word.

Psalm 145:4

Psalm 112:1-3

30

GO FORTH AND WAGE WAR

The righteous who walks in his integrity—
blessed are his children after him!

PROVERBS 20:7

We've been tasked with a great responsibility. And as Jesus said, to whom much is given, much is required. In the large view, this can seem overwhelming and intimidating. But we must move forward. There's too much at stake to stay where we are.

Karl Wallenda, a German-born daredevil, once walked a high wire across Tallulah Gorge (a thousand feet deep and a quarter-mile wide) in northeast Georgia. Before his stunt, he was asked if he thought he could make it. He responded: "If I make my first three steps, you will know I am going to make it. That's the hard part, those first three steps."

If we can muster enough courage to take the first few steps in spiritually leading our families, we'll have the momentum to carry us the rest of the way. My hope and prayer is that this devotional has created a spark in your heart that will ignite a fire deep in your soul for the spiritual upbringing of your children. We can no longer be passive. We must wage war against the enemy and intentionally and fervently build our children into the men and women God has called them to be. We must stand firm, knowing that the moment we begin directing our families toward Christ, the devil will look to cut us down at every opportunity. He'll make you feel unqualified. He'll spout lies of failure and attack your pride. He'll try to create chaos in your marriage and cause division between you and your children. Immerse yourself in the truths of Scripture, spend time in your own relationship with Jesus, and lead your family with conviction and purpose.

As someone once said, "My hope is that when I die, all of hell rejoices that I'm out of the fight." What a powerful statement! Imagine being such a force that hell itself rejoices when you've stepped into the glory of the King! My only addition to that statement is that the rejoicing of hell will quickly turn to fear, because my offspring and the generations after me are assembling for war—they're approaching the gates of hell, and those gates will not prevail.

We're called to be warriors, and our children are like arrows in our hands. May we raise them to fly true, released into this world with the power of the Holy Spirit, and being led by the razor-sharp truth of God's Holy Word.

May we stay humble, stay focused, and keep pressing onward, fighting the good fight, and changing the world one generation at a time!

As the character Maximus said in the film *The Gladiator*, "Brothers, what we do in this life will echo in eternity."

THE ARMORY

Romans 5:3-5

Nehemiah 4:14

Isaiah 43:1-3

CPSIA information can be obtained
at www.ICGtesting.com
Printed in the USA
JSHW050806150622
27032JS00004B/14